W9-BWF-345

598.34
SWI
c.1 Switzer, Merebeth
    Flamingos

OUR WILDLIFE WORLD

FLAMINGOS

Merebeth Switzer

 Grolier

FACTS IN BRIEF

Classification of Flamingos
Class: Aves(birds)
Order: Phoenicopteriformes(flamingo)
Family: Phoenicopteridae
Genus: There are 3 genera of flamingos.
Species: There are 5 species (and one sub-species) of flamingos.

World distribution.   Southern Eurasia, Africa, Caribbean, Mexico, South America and the Galapagos Islands.

Habitat.   Lagoons, marshes and mud flats near oceans or seas.

Distinctive physical characteristics. Tall pink bird with a long neck and legs, and a thick, bent pink beak with a black tip.

Habits.   Gathers in colonies of thousands of birds. Usually flies at night to feeding or breeding spots. Good swimmer.

Diet. Tiny aquatic plants and animals.

Published originally as
"Getting to Know . . . Nature's Children."

This series is approved and recommended
by the Federation of Ontario Naturalists.

Canadian Cataloguing in Publication Data

Switzer, Merebeth.
  Flamingos

(Our wildlife world)
ISBN 0-7172-2659-X

1. Flamingos—Juvenile literature.
I. Title.   II. Series.

QL696.C56S8 1990   j598'.34   C90-095095-1

Contents

Imagine yourself paddling along the edge of a tropical marsh at sunset. Your canoe glides peacefully over the calm water. There silhouetted against the sunset is a great flock of beautiful, long-legged pink birds. Flamingos!

At the outside edges of the group stand a few birds who warily eye your approach. These are sentinels, standing guard against intruders. If you want to get closer, you must move ever so slowly and quietly. Otherwise they will take to the air in a rush of noise and movement and settle somewhere far away from any onlookers.

Exactly what do you know about these tall elegant birds? You already know that flamingos are pink, but did you realize that flamingo parents feed their offspring a kind of "milk," or that sometimes flamingos can lose their pinkness? Let's find out more about these amazing birds.

Are You My Mom?

Hundreds of flamingos stand quietly in the water. Most are asleep, dozing with their heads tucked under their wing. In the middle of one group, a gangly little gray chick scurries from bird to bird, pecking at one pair of legs after another. Each grownup grunts or squawks a complaint at this rude awakening. The chick listens.

In this big flock of look-alike pink birds, the chick will only be able to know its real parents by their voices. Each honk-like squawk is different and tells the youngster that this bird is not one of its parents. But wait a minute, there is the sound! The bird that has just woken up bends its long neck down in greeting and the chick now takes a safe stand between its mother's legs.

Hello down there. (Greater Flamingo)

The Flamingo Family

There are six different kinds of flamingos and they are found in many parts of the world. The most widespread is the Greater Flamingo, which lives and breeds in southern Europe, parts of Asia and Africa. The Lesser Flamingo, which outnumbers all its relatives, is found in Africa south of the Sahara. The other four types of flamingos have small ranges. The Caribbean Flamingo lives on islands in the Caribbean, in Mexico and on the Galapagos Islands. The Chilean Flamingo is found along the western coast of South America while the Andean and James' flamingos live near salt lakes high up in the hills in central South America.

Opposite page: *Caribbean Flamingo.*

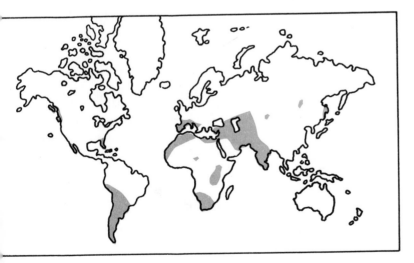

The shaded areas on this map show where flamingos are found.

9

Family Reunion

Scientists can't seem to agree on just what kinds of birds are related to the flamingo. Because of the similarity in appearance, some people believe that long-legged herons and storks are their closest relatives. Also their offspring and some of the feathers seem to be a close match. Other bird specialists point to the connection between waterfowl, such as ducks, geese and swans, and flamingos. They all have webbed feet, they swim well and they fly in similar patterns. Besides, their chicks behave the same way. Another group of scientists disagrees with both these suggestions and instead notes the things wading birds, like the oyster catcher, and flamingos have in common. After all, they have similar skeletons and behavior.

Just which birds *are* related to flamingos? No one is certain, and so it would seem that these tall pink birds had best postpone the family reunion until all the scientists can agree.

Unlike some other long-legged birds, flamingos are good swimmers.

A Marshy Home

Flamingos are warm-weather birds and they are found only in the tropics and subtropics. They prefer lagoons, swampy areas and marshes that border on saltwater.

These lagoons, marshes and swamps can be quite salty themselves. Now, if you have ever sipped saltwater or sat in the ocean for any length of time, you may wonder about this choice. Saltwater is unpleasant to drink and it dries your skin and makes it itchy. But flamingos do not come to these marshes in search of water to drink or bathe in. They come to be near their food — tiny, little plants and shellfish that live in saltwater or somewhat salty, brackish water. They drink the freshwater they can find in springs — even steaming hot ones will do — or in puddles after a rainfall.

There's always room for another flamingo at the feeding ground.

Sifting for Supper

The flamingo's beak is specially designed to allow it to sift out tiny little sea creatures and plants from the water.

To do this, the flamingo swishes its head, upside down, back and forth in the water. While doing so, it moves its fleshy tongue back and forth to bring water into its mouth, and then to force it back out. And it does this at an amazing speed, sucking in water and pushing it out up to 20 times a second! Bristles along the upper and lower part of its beak trap the bits of food as the water comes squirting out. In other words, the bristles filter the food from the water, and so flamingos are called filter feeders.

Depending on what they like to eat, some flamingos have rows of big bristles in their beaks and others have much finer bristles. For instance, the Greater Flamingo with its larger bristles traps small snails and insects 2.5 centimetres (an inch) long for dinner. The Lesser Flamingo with its smaller bristles captures tiny plants and animals that you can only see with the help of a microscope.

Opposite page:
The flamingo's bent beak is one of the most specialized beaks in the world.

Stirring the Pot

If you were lying undercover, watching flamingos feeding, you would wonder about the strange dance that they were doing. Look, there's one now, stamping its feet up and down as it swishes its beak back and forth in the water.

The flamingo is stirring up its dinner. By disturbing the mud, it stirs up the little plants and animals that live there. When they are floating around in the water, it's a lot easier for the flamingo to sift them out for a meal.

Flamingos that eat relatively large creatures dip their heads quite deep into the water, whereas those that eat the tiniest creatures often feed just below the surface. Since different flamingos eat different sized food, you can often see two types dining happily together.

Mmm . . . a nice, wet dinner.

In the Pink

A flock made up of thousands of very large, pink birds is truly an amazing sight. No matter what the species of flamingo, it is some kind of pink. Greater Flamingos are various shades of soft pink with pink legs and feet. Caribbean Flamingos are much more colorful. Their upper feathers are bright scarlet, while their tummies and underwings are a slightly lighter shade. Like all flamingos they have black flight feathers and a black tipped beak.

But why are flamingos pink? It seems such a strange color for a big bird.

Flamingos get their color from natural red dyes that occur in the shrimp-like creatures that they eat. If you have ever peeled a lot of carrots and then looked at your hands afterwards, you know just how effectively this kind of natural dye can stain! People only discovered the reason for the flamingo's rosy color when some kept in a zoo turned almost white because they were missing the special dye from their diet.

Pink, beautiful pink.

Tall, Taller, Tallest

Flamingos vary somewhat in size depending on their species. The smallest are the James' Flamingo and the Lesser Flamingo. They grow to about the height of an average six-year old — 120 centimetres (48 inches) or so. Mind you, that's still pretty tall for a bird. The tallest in the western hemisphere is the Caribbean Flamingo. At 160 centimetres (62 inches) it is only slightly smaller than its eastern counterpart, the Greater Flamingo.

Surprisingly, for all their height flamingos are very light. Even the biggest weigh no more than 4 kilograms (9 pounds). Or maybe not so surprising since all the height is made up of legs and neck.

Bet you wouldn't be able to do this for long.

Birds of a Feather

Feathers are very important to all birds. They are one of the things that they have in common with one another, and they are one of the things that make a bird a bird.

Like most birds, flamingos have four basic types of feathers. The small, fluffy down feathers against the body help to keep the bird warm and make it as waterproof as possible. Tail feathers, which are longer and stiffer, are used for steering in the air, balance on the ground and also for some courtship rituals to impress a mate. To smooth the flow of air over the wings inner wing feathers are needed. Finally, the strong outer wing feathers provide the power for flight.

You'd best keep your distance from a wet flamingo unless you're ready to get wet too!

Feather Care

A flamingo's feathers go through a lot of wear and tear in a year. Unlike you, the flamingo can't just go out and get a new coat. Instead it grows a whole new set of feathers. How often it does so depends to some extent on how old the bird is and whether or not it has had any offspring that year. On average, flamingos molt about once every 12 months, though some types may shed twice in one year, growing first a set of rather pale feathers and later a darker pink set. The process is usually a gradual one with old feathers being replaced a few at a time by new ones. But once in a while a flamingo may molt so quickly that it is unable to fly for a few weeks. This is a dangerous and nerve-wracking time for the grounded bird.

And how does the flamingo care for its new feathers? It spends a lot of time preening. This involves ruffling its wings and tail in the water and air, using its beak like a comb and spreading the natural oils present along the length of its feathers. It even uses its feet to give its head feathers a good scratch once in a while.

Night Flights

We usually picture flamingos standing, on one leg or two, in a marsh or in shallow water. But flamingos are very strong fliers and they can travel great distances without landing for a rest.

Because their wings are so big, however, flamingos cannot change directions easily. This means that they are easy targets for big birds of prey, like the Fish Eagle. With these and other hunters around, it is not safe for flamingos to fly in the open. Understandably reluctant to end up as a meal for a hawk or eagle, flamingos fly from feeding ground to feeding ground at night, when most birds of prey are asleep.

Flamingos fly at an average speed of 55 kilometres (34 miles) per hour.

On the Alert

Opposite page:

Resting flamingos often face into the wind to help them keep their balance.

Flamingos may snooze at any time of the day or night. But, a sleeping flamingo does not always look like a bird at rest. By our standards, in fact, it sometimes looks downright uncomfortable. Flamingos frequently sleep standing up, often on one leg, with their long neck curled up and their head tucked under one wing.

Why would the flamingo choose such an awkward sleeping position? For some very good reasons. The most important one seems to be that it finds it perfectly comfortable. Also if a flamingo sleeps standing up, it can quickly fly off if a hungry predator approaches. Standing on one leg conserves body heat as well. If you've ever spent a long time in water you know how it cools your body. By standing on one leg, the flamingo keeps all but the smallest part of the body from being cooled by the water.

Of course, flamingos don't always sleep standing up. They sometimes sit down on dry land and, when they have an egg in their nest, they spend a lot of time sitting dozily on it to keep it warm.

On the look-out for a mate.

Honk Honk

What would you expect to see if you heard a great bunch of birds honking overhead? Probably not a flock of flamingos flying by with their necks stretched out in front and their pink legs dangling behind. But it could happen if you were in the right place. Flamingos sound quite a bit like geese and you would not be the first person to make that mistake.

During the mating season, when males and females are looking for a partner, they make a lot of other noises too. The male works hard to impress the female that appeals to him, and he makes many goose-like love honks and gabbling sounds to attract her attention. If she is interested, she will honk back at him, then they will both honk. Some types of flamingos will then run back and forth in groups with their heads high in the air. Then they may shake them from side to side while calling loudly and open their large wings all at once. Other flamingos separate into pairs before beginning the courtship dance.

Starting A Family

Starting A Family

Opposite page:
*A flamingo nest
under
construction.
(Chilean
Flamingo)*

Flamingos are very social birds, and even when they are nesting they are found in large flocks. They build their nests close together in shallow water or on the open stretches of mud flats that sometimes appear when the water level of a lake or marsh drops. Sometimes flamingos will build on small rocky islands in salt lagoons if other nesting sites are lacking.

The flamingo's nest does not provide the kind of warm snug home many birds build for new chicks. The nests are amazing structures, tall cones of mud with flattened tops. To build these nests takes a lot of work and patience. Soon after she has a mate the mother flamingo chooses a nesting site and usually begins the process. She rakes up mud into a pile, then stomps on it and pats it with her beak to make the base of the nest mound. As the mound gets higher, she uses her beak to carry more dollops of mud for the top and sides. Then she hops up on top to pack the mud into place in order to make a good solid nest. By the time she is finished, the nest could be up to 40 centimetres (16 inches) tall.

Finishing Touches

The father flamingo generally helps out once the basic mud mound is complete. He helps to hollow out the top into a bowl-like shape. Having the nest slope down toward the center prevents the egg or eggs from rolling out. Pebbles, grass, shells and more mud is gathered around the base of the mound until the birds are satisfied that the nest is strong and safe.

Sometimes flamingos are forced to nest where mud is scarce. In this case, the nest is a small mound of grass and gravel. But the flamingos still build a low protecting wall of clay pellets packed together around it.

You may be wondering why flamingos build such unusual nests. They have their reasons. Living near water can be tricky — water levels change and storms can cause flooding. The tall mound keeps the egg(s) high and dry.

Keeping an eye on Junior.

Hatching Time

On the round dish-like top of their nest, flamingos lay one, or sometimes two, white chalky eggs. It takes a month for the eggs to hatch, and during this time both the male and female take turns sitting on the nest. They turn the egg frequently to make sure that the chick inside develops evenly and that it doesn't stick to the sides of the shell. At some point as the babies develop inside the eggs, they begin to hear the sounds their parents make. By the time they hatch, they know their parents' voices.

When the chick is ready to hatch, it begins to peep. Then it starts breaking through the eggshell with a special little point on its beak called an egg tooth. It sometimes takes the hatchling 24 hours or longer to break out of the hard shell. In the meantime, the parents stay very close with their beaks almost touching the egg, making encouraging noises.

A flamingo chick gets a lot of attention from its parents.

The "Ugly Ducking"

A flamingo chick is quite an unexpected sight. It has the same body shape as its parents, including a very long neck and a pair of long gangly legs. But it is covered in fluffy, pale gray down, and its straight pinkish-red beak is nothing like that of its parents. It will be several weeks in fact before the chick's beak even begins to get the characteristic curve of an adult flamingo's. Not surprisingly, people often ask what those "strange-looking gray birds" are that they sometimes see with flamingo flocks.

Within a week after it hatches the chick is ready to venture out of the nest for a short walk or swim. The parents follow along anxiously ready to defend their baby from the slightest harm. With both mom and dad tagging along the young chick is very well protected.

You can tell that this chick is more than a month old because it is covered in gray downy plumage and its beak is beginning to bend downwards.

Flamingo Milk

Flamingo parents are kept busy feeding their youngster for the first while after it hatches. Fortunately their nest is always near their feeding area.

To feed the chick, the parent must stand behind it and lower its neck and its head upside down. For the first month of its life the flamingo chick feeds on special red-colored "milk" from its parents. This flamingo milk is rich in fats and comes from the cells on the inside of the bird's crop. (The crop is a special organ that helps it to grind up its food.) The chick clasps the parent's beak and drinks the milk, rather like a human baby sucking on a bottle.

The young flamingo grows quickly on this nourishing liquid. By the time it is a month old, feathers begin to appear on its wings and body. Soon after that its beak begins to turn down just like its parents' beaks.

Both male and female flamingos feed and care for their fluffy offspring. (Andean Flamingos)

Day Care

Flamingo chicks love crowds just as their parents do. They trot around on their own at a very young age and gather together in large groups called creches. But they are never left alone. At least one chick's parents are nearby to lead the group away from danger or to discourage any predator that might be looking for a meal. In parts of Africa, this might be a Fish Eagle, hyena, cheetah or jackal. In some places it might even be an alligator or a crocodile.

On the ground, the adults are very good at protecting their young and themselves from predators. They charge at intruders, growling and flapping their large, strong wings. Their wings can be surprisingly dangerous and can do serious damage to any animal that gets too close.

After lunch, the mother flamingo will probably spend some time preening her chick's feathers.

Growing Up

By the time it is three months old the flamingo chick has learned how to fly by watching its parents and other flamingos. Of course it takes quite a bit of practice to manoeuvre its large wings and to keep its legs and neck out of the way. It has also learned how to filter feed properly and only occasionally begs for food from its parents.

Before its first birthday, the young flamingo has grown a new set of pale feathers. Not until it is 3 or 4 years old will it have a complete pink set. Young flamingos are ready to start a family at the age of 6, and with luck they may live and breed for 20 or 25 years in the salty waters of the world.

Words to Know

Chick   A young bird before or after hatching.

Creche   A large group of young flamingo chicks that is watched over by at least one set of parents.

Crop   Part of a bird's food passage where food is prepared for digestion.

Down   Short, soft feathers that cover young birds or underlie the outer feathers of adult birds.

Egg tooth   A tooth-like point on a chick's bill used to help it crack out of its egg.

Hatch   To emerge from an egg.

Hatchling   A chick that is breaking out or has just broken out of the egg.

Mate   To come together to produce young. Either member of an animal pair is also the other's mate.

Molt   To shed feathers, skin, shell or horns periodically before a new growth.

Predator   An animal that hunts other animals for food.

Preening   Cleaning and oiling the feathers.

INDEX

Cover Photo: Phyllis Greenberg
Photo Credits: John Moss (Photo Researchers, Inc.), page 4; M.P. Kahl, pages 7, 12, 19, 28, 43; Bill Ivy, pages 8, 11, 16, 23, 24, 27, 31, 32; Stan Bain, pages 14, 15; Boyd Norton, page 20; New York Zoological Society, page 36; Zoological Society of San Diego, page 39; E. Bartels, page 40; Academy of Natural Sciences of Philadelphia, page 44.